**Walks in the High**

# The
# High Street Fells

by
Tom Bowker

Dalesman Books
1991

The Dalesman Publishing Company Ltd.,
Clapham, via Lancaster, LA2 8EB

First published 1991

ISBN: 1 85568 023 8

Printed by Peter Fretwell & Sons Ltd., Goulbourne Street, Keighley, West Yorkshire.

# Contents

*Sketch maps by Tom Bowker*

# Key to Maps

△ GREY CRAG     a ridge crowned by a summit

A592     a road or walled lane

a tarn and exit beck

a lake

woodland

line of walk described

building, sheepfold, etc.

footbridge over a beck

wall or fence that is particularly useful for navigation

cairn, cave, natural landmarks, or other points of interest

hause or saddle in a ridge

P     parking area or start of walk

# Introduction

THIS third book in a series offers walks on the High Street fells, a title under which I embrace all the two thousand foot summits east of the A592 Windermere – Penrith and west of the A6, ranging from Loadpot Hill in the north to Yoke in the south.

I've arranged the walks under sub-titles e.g. 'High Street (South)', which means the walk either starts south of an imaginary line drawn east-to-west through High Street summit and climbs to that summit, or lies in an area south of that line; or 'High Street (East)', which means the walk either starts east of an imaginary line drawn north-to-south through High Street summit and climbs to that summit, or lies in an area east of that line. Also included, as a bonus for the fellwalker who likes a challenge, is a 'marathon' circuit of the four highest mountains in Lakeland. As a guidebook writer I feel myself torn between an eagerness to introduce readers to my beloved Lakeland fells, a natural desire that my books will sell, and a concern that I must accept some blame for the consequent erosion of mountain paths. With the latter in mind I try to diverge from the mountain 'motorways', thus hoping to spread the load a little.

The walks described should be treated with due respect. Boots should be worn and rucksacks should contain waterproofs, spare clothing, map, compass, whistle and survival bag. In winter a torch, balaclava, mittens and some extra food should be added. When snow and ice coat the fells an ice-axe should be carried. Crampons are becoming more commonly used by fellwalkers, and rightly so. Frequent practice in the use of map and compass make that winter day when their use suddenly becomes vital much less terrifying. Remember the cardinal rule – start using your compass from a point where you know where you are, don't wait until you are lost. Successful navigation through deteriorating conditions adds a bonus to your day and a boost to your confidence. Remember, in an emergency, all becks flow downhill and if followed with care can be fast escape routes in bad weather. Never be afraid to turn back. The fells will still be there next weekend.

Alongside each walk, except for the 'marathon', is a sketch map to be used in conjunction with the text. It is advisable, however, also to carry the relevant sheet of the 1:25000 The English Lakes Outdoor Leisure Maps. All the place names in the text refer to the 1982 edition of these maps. The mileages and heights of ascent are approximate and 'left' or 'right' refers to a physical feature as if facing it. Parking details are as per the maps, local authorities and tradition up to press, but are always liable to change. Limited space means I have to choose between detailed route descriptions, incidental information, and detailed descriptions of views. I tend to be niggardly with the latter, feeling it's useful for walkers to attempt to orientate the view to their map.

The only way to learn about the fells is to be out regularly in all conditions. There will be times when you are frightened and times when you are physically exhausted. Ironically, these are the days that live most vividly in the memory and when you learn something about the mountains. Don't forget that it's a game, it's fun, it's adventure. For the fellwalker, given reasonable fitness and equipment, using his/her commonsense, the dangers are more apparent than real. Statistically, you are probably in more danger in your home or on your journey to and from the fells.

The Lakeland fells have become inextricably woven into the weft of my life. My addiction to climbing them led to love, marriage and fatherhood, and innumerable friendships. They stimulated my interest in writing and are the bedrock of its continuing development. They have given me untold days of rewarding physical endeavour, good company, and wonderment at the beauty seen. If this booklet should bring such pleasures to any who read it I will be content. Happy walking!

**Tom Bowker**

# HIGH STREET (SOUTH)

**Walk 1**                                **11 miles**
**3500 feet of ascent**

# A Troutbeck Round

*The outward leg of this walk crosses some of the fine, but oftimes crowded, peaks of the popular Kentmere Horseshoe. In contrast, the return trip climbs an entertaining, but less busy, peak and descends into and down a lonely valley where the discerning will discover interesting relics of a past Lakeland.*

*Parking: In the layby on the western verge of the A592 Windermere-Penrith road, above the entrance to the Limefitt Caravan & Camping Site, Troutbeck. (GR 414031).*

GO through the entrance to the campsite. Follow the road through the site towards the farm. Just below it turn left by a multi-armed signpost. Walk past the ablutions block before turning right to pass through a gap in a wall. Turn left to pass through a metal gate and climb up to join a crossing path. Turn left, then almost immediately right up a path slanting up the steep fellside towards a plantation. A steep pull leads to a stile leading on to the Garburn Road. Turn left and follow this ancient mountain highway to the gate just beyond the crest of Garburn Pass. Go through the gate and turn left alongside a wall.

From Garburn Pass the way over the fine trio of Yoke, 2316 feet, Ill Bell, 2483 feet, and Froswick, 2363 feet, is obvious and needs no description, a worn path being beaten into the hide of the fells by the passage of zillions of boots. Shapely peak follows shapely peak, the ground falls away steeply on either hand, and the views of lake and fell are widespread and constantly changing. It is Lakeland fellwalking at its best, especially on a sunny winter day with a pelt of crisp snow underfoot. (See Walk 2 regarding 'dog-legs' in the ridge after Ill Bell and Froswick.)

Beyond Froswick the ridge climbs to join the High Street massif near an old iron fencepost embedded in a sizeable rock, where paths fork. Climb left, north-westerly, to meet a tail of crumbling wall leading up to the splendid chimney-like cairn crowning Thornthwaite Crag, 2572 feet, the high point of the walk. Southwards are glimmering miles of isle-cluttered Windermere, but northwards only the fell-shadowed head of Ullswater peers around Place Fell. Fanning westward are a mighty army of fells and the task of identifying them will give you every excuse for a breather in the lee of the cairn.

From the cairn keep to the west (left) side of the wall descending in a north-to-westerly curve on to the grassy saddle of Threshthwaite Mouth. It develops into a steep descent over rough ground and care should be taken in winter conditions. Follow the wall across the saddle to the foot of the steep rocky flank of Stony Cove Pike. (From here a path dropping left offers a safe escape route back into the Troutbeck Valley should you need it). If not, follow the wall in a surprisingly rocky climb in this enclave of largely grassy fells. When the angle eases out on to the broad grassy summit dome of Stony Cove Pike, 2503 feet, the path veers left (south-west) away from the wall to reach the accepted summit cairn, though several surrounding bumps look equally as high.

The faint path heads south-west from the cairn to a gap in the wall. Do not go through this gap. Turn left and follow the wall down the south ridge of Stony Cove Pike to meet ultimately a crossing wall. Climb over the crossing wall and continue down to reach the bank of a rocky beck cascading gradually leftwards to a junction with the Trout Beck on the boggy valley floor. Scramble down alongside it, enjoying the waterfalls, to meet the 'escape' path from Threshthwaite Mouth (previously described) where it crosses your descending beck. Turn right along it, across the beck, to reach a stile in a stone wall. Cross the stile and follow the narrow path wending down the valley of the Trout Beck, between a craggy spur of Stony Cove Pike and the grassy ridge of The Tongue. Keep your eyes open for two circular drystone grassy-topped platforms to the right of this path. These are 'pitsteads', relics of the days when charcoal burners, or 'colliers', used to bivouac around these platforms on which they built their fires to produce charcoal for the gunpowder mills. You may also spot deer on the slopes of The Tongue, if you are lucky.

About a mile from the stile look for a solidly-constructed stone footbridge spanning the Trout Beck. Cross this and follow the path on the far bank above a waterfall and ultimately down to the rear of Troutbeck Park Farm. Go to the right of the buildings then turn left in front of the farmhouse on to the farm road. Follow this down the valley. Where it turns right to climb up on to the A592 keep straight on up a narrow 'Public Bridleway' which ultimately brings you onto the A592 just a few hundred yards above your car.

WARNING. This path debouches abruptly on to an often busy road. Take heed of the traffic before you step out.

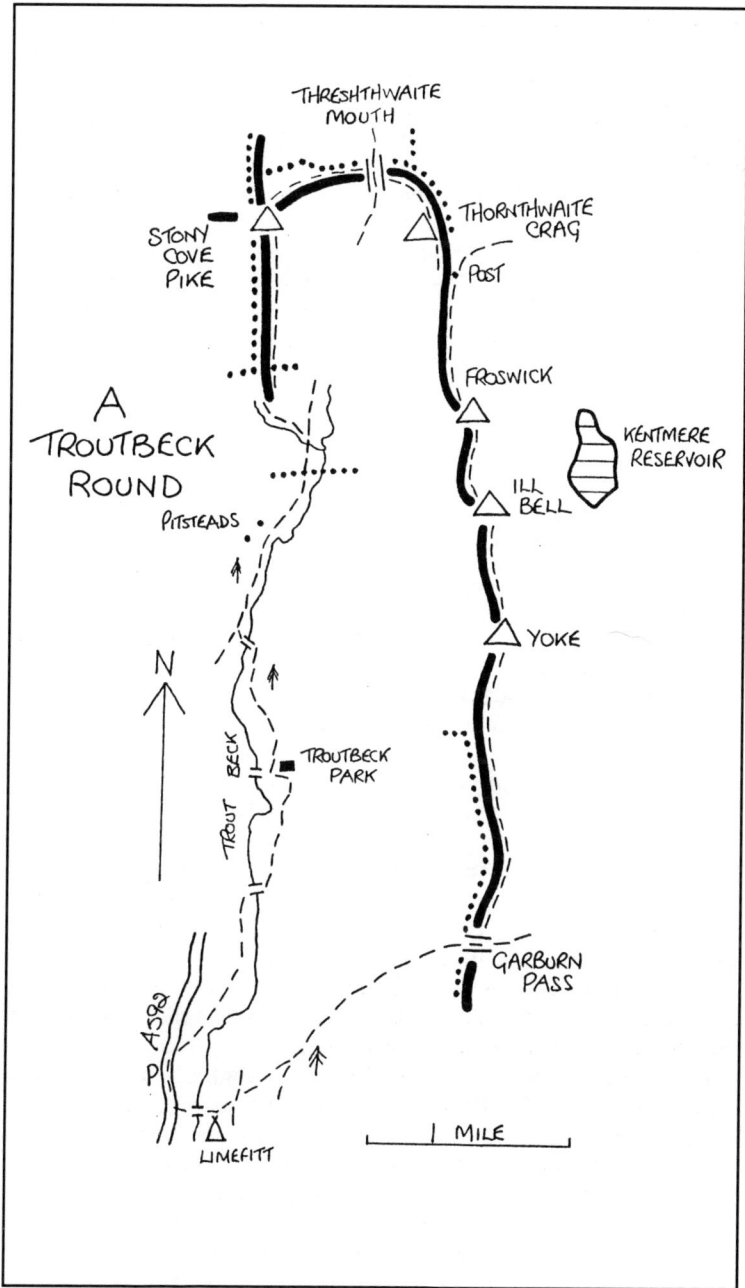

A
TROUTBECK
ROUND

THRESHTHWAITE MOUTH

STONY COVE PIKE

THORNTHWAITE CRAG

POST

FROSWICK

KENTMERE RESERVOIR

ILL BELL

PITSTEADS

N

TROUT BECK

YOKE

TROUTBECK PARK

GARBURN PASS

A592

P

LIMEFITT

MILE

# A Variation on the Kentmere Horseshoe

*The Kentmere Horseshoe is one of Lakeland's most popular walks,
now unfortunately paying the penalty for its popularity, becoming
rutted and scarred by the passage of countless boots. The walk
described below takes in the most interesting parts of the original
horseshoe yet makes a gesture towards footpath conservation by
offering a different start and finish that are themselves interesting.*

*Parking: Always a problem with space being limited and the walk so
popular. At the time of writing the only answer is to arrive early and
'bag' one of the spaces available near Kentmere Church. (GR 456041).*

WALK back along the road, around the corner, down to then left up
the farm track behind the church. Turn right at the fork eventually to
pass in front of the dwelling at Rook House (gate). Once over the rise
beyond look for a stile in the wall to your right leading to a footbridge
over the River Kent. Climb the far bank to a stile leading into walled
Low Lane. Turn left along the lane to where paths fork beyond a
clapper bridge (a stone slab, or slabs, spanning a beck). Take the left
fork, signposted 'Public Bridleway – Mardale'. Beyond the wall and
fields to your left Yoke, Ill Bell, and Froswick tower craggily over still
hidden Kentmere Reservoir. When the path climbs right, towards a
farm, turn left, past a telegraph pole, to a gate. Beyond the gate a
grassy, occasionally boggy, path leads to a gate opening on to a
tarmac road near Overend Farm. Turn left and down past the farm
gate on to a path signposted 'Public Footpath – Kentmere Reservoir'.
    This leads pleasantly through fields to derelict Tongue House. Go
around to the right and behind the ruin to a gate. Turn right beyond
this and around the foot of Tongue Scar to a stile. Cross this on to a
flattish grassy area between disused quarries and the river. Across
the river looms quarry-pocked Rainsbarrow Crag. Cross the river by
stepping stones to join the rough track climbing right towards
Kentmere Reservoir. (If the crossing is impassable follow the right
bank of the river to cross the dam, or ford the Kent above the
reservoir.) Otherwise, follow the track along the west bank of the
reservoir. After rounding a rocky point the now fading path climbs
left across the base of a grassy ridge. Climb left up this steepening
ridge on to its easier-angled and more defined continuation. The
final rocky headwall is steep but the only real difficulty to overcome

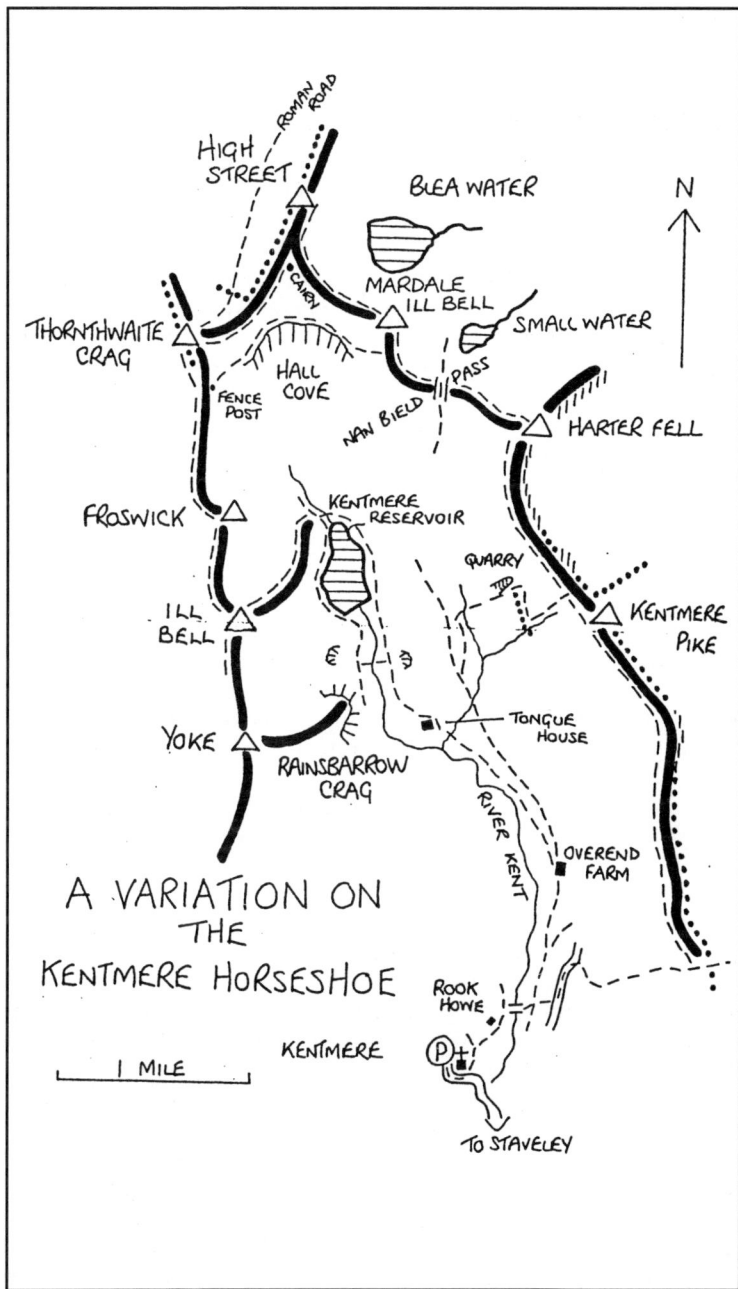

HIGH STREET

ROMAN ROAD

BLEA WATER

N

MARDALE ILL BELL

SMALL WATER

CAIRN

THORNTHWAITE CRAG

HALL COVE

NAN BIELD PASS

HARTER FELL

FENCE POST

FROSWICK

KENTMERE RESERVOIR

QUARRY

ILL BELL

KENTMERE PIKE

YOKE

RAINSBARROW CRAG

TONGUE HOUSE

RIVER KENT

OVEREND FARM

A VARIATION ON THE KENTMERE HORSESHOE

ROOK HOWE

KENTMERE

1 MILE

TO STAVELEY

before the triple-cairned summit of Ill Bell, 2483 feet, is reached, is a severe shortage of breath.

Now follow the eroded 'horseshoe' path north-westerly down the summit rocks into the dip below the grassy ridge climbing onto Froswick, 2363 feet. The High Street dome dominates the view ahead, with the chimney-like cairn crowning Thornthwaite Crag to its left. Look left and below this for a glint of Ullswater beyond the saddle of Threshthwaite Mouth. Again, a north-westerly descent leads into the next, boggy, dip in the ridge. (In mist, or 'white-out', it's useful to remember that the main ridge side-steps west just beyond the summits of both Ill Bell and Froswick.) Now climb the grassy ridge beyond, passing isolated fenceposts. A prominent fencepost embedded in a large boulder marks an important path fork. The right fork offers an easier alternative, leading around the rim of Hall Cove and ultimately down on to Nan Bield Pass. Unless you are forced by time, unfitness, or weather to take this route follow the left fork, climbing north-westerly to meet a length of crumbling wall leading up to the splendid cairn crowning Thornthwaite Crag, 2572 feet. It will be highly unusual if you do not find other walkers enjoying a 'breather' in the lee of the cairn or its supporting wall, for it's a kind of Piccadilly Circus in this complex of grassy cones and domes.

Descend east, then north-east, across a broad grassy saddle tilting into the Hayeswater combe, and on up to a wall corner. Ignore the path breaching the wall, which follows the line of the 'Roman Road' and passes to the west of the High Street summit. Walk to the right of the corner and climb alongside the wall ultimately to reach the trig-point crowning High Street, 2716 feet. (En route, note a cairn to the right of the wall marking a path fork. This is the starting point of your return leg.) Given a clear day walk north-easterly from the trig-point to a cairn on the fell rim for a 'birds-eye' view of Blea Water, whose over two hundred foot depth make it Lakeland's deepest tarn; Riggindale, the lair of Lakeland's Golden Eagles; and distant Haweswater.

Return to the trig-point and descend back down to the cairn previously mentioned. Turn left here to descend south-easterly over broad grasslands into the dip below Mardale Ill Bell, 2493 feet. (In a 'white-out' it would be wise to take a compass bearing for these amiable slopes fall precipitously away on either hand. Given a clear day walk left from the dip and you'll see what I mean!) From Mardale Ill Bell a good path twists down rockier ground to the shelter crowning Nan Bield Pass. Climb its far slope, a steepish rocky ridge, and sooner than you think you'll be standing by the piled stones and rusting fenceposts crowning Harter Fell, 2552 feet. Far to the west Gable's dome predominates, with the sliced-off summit of Pillar to its right and the high jumble of the Scafells to its left.

The final leg of the Kentmere Horseshoe presents no problems with navigation or terrain. A fence, or sometimes a wall, initially descending south-south-westerly, follows the crest of the ridge over Kentmere Pike, 2394 feet, (the trig-point lies over the wall) and Shipman Knotts to debouch, just over three miles later, on to the public bridleway linking Kentmere and Longsleddale. Turn right here and down on to the tarmac of High Lane. Follow this left to a stile on your right signposted 'Kentmere'. Cross this and the field beyond to a stile leading into Low Lane opposite the stile of your outward route.

VARIATION FINISH. Initially steeper and rougher, but interesting. From Harter Fell top follow the fence/wall into the dip below Kentmere Pike. Now turn right and follow boggy runnels down to a spring. Continue down steepening ground to the right of a beck which cascades into a rocky gill. Slant right, then left, down slabby rocks to the foot of the gill. Now make an undulating traverse right, across the fellside, alongside an old wall, which eventually leads down to the foot of an impressive derelict quarry whose sheer, smooth walls enclose a fine waterfall. Follow the wall below the spoil heaps down to Ullstone Gill. Cross the gill and follow a path down the far bank to a junction with the public bridleway descending from Nan Bield. Turn left and follow this pleasantly down to a junction with your outward route at Overend Farm.

# A Longsleddale Round

*Although one of the most accessible of Lakeland valleys, from the
south, Longsleddale retains an air of rugged isolation, especially in
winter. The summits rising above its north-eastern flank are largely
unfrequented, even in summer. Hereabouts, the broad shouldered
Pennine takes over from the more starkly sculpted Cumbrian. The
summits may be dull but there is much of interest tucked into the rocky
flanks and corners of these fells.*

*Parking: Near Sadgill Bridge, Longsleddale, where the 'slate' road
begins. (GR 484057).*

WALK up the 'slate' road. Buckbarrow Crag rises impressively
ahead, and as you approach you will see that it is split into an upper
and lower crag by a roughly zig-zagging grass terrace. This is the
'climbers way down' and your line of ascent. Cross the stile in the wall
below the foot of the crag and climb steep grass and scree to reach the
foot of an obvious gully, Cleft Ghyll, splitting the upper crag. Climb
the grassy ledges slanting left from the foot of Cleft Ghyll and above
the rocks of the lower crag. These ledges zig-zag right, then left,
under crags, to end in grassy grooves at the left hand edge of the
upper crag. (A popular climb called Dandle Buttress runs up the
right bounding wall of Cleft Ghyll. From the 'climbers way down' it
shows as a towering, spiky pinnacle and provides a 'scoop' for
photographers if there are climbers clinging to it.)

Scramble up the steepish grassy grooves at the edge of the upper
crag on to amiable grass slopes. An easterly heading leads to a fence
below a belt of low crags guarding the summit of the fell. Cross the
fence and scramble through the crags to reach the crumbling survey
pillar, used in the construction of the Haweswater Reservoir,
dominating the broad grassy summit of Tarn Crag, 2178 feet. The
insignificant cairn lies a few paces beyond. (Eager peakbaggers could
now make an out-and-back foray to the south-east to 'bag' Grey
Crag, 2093 feet, the most easterly of Lakeland's two-thousand footers.)

From Tarn Crag head north-easterly to meet a fence then follow
it north-westerly then north down to the gate crowning the saddle at
the head of the lonely valley of Mosedale. Keep your eyes peeled, for
this is deer country. Follow the fence up the far slope to join a wall
which is followed to a junction with a fence on the grassy summit of

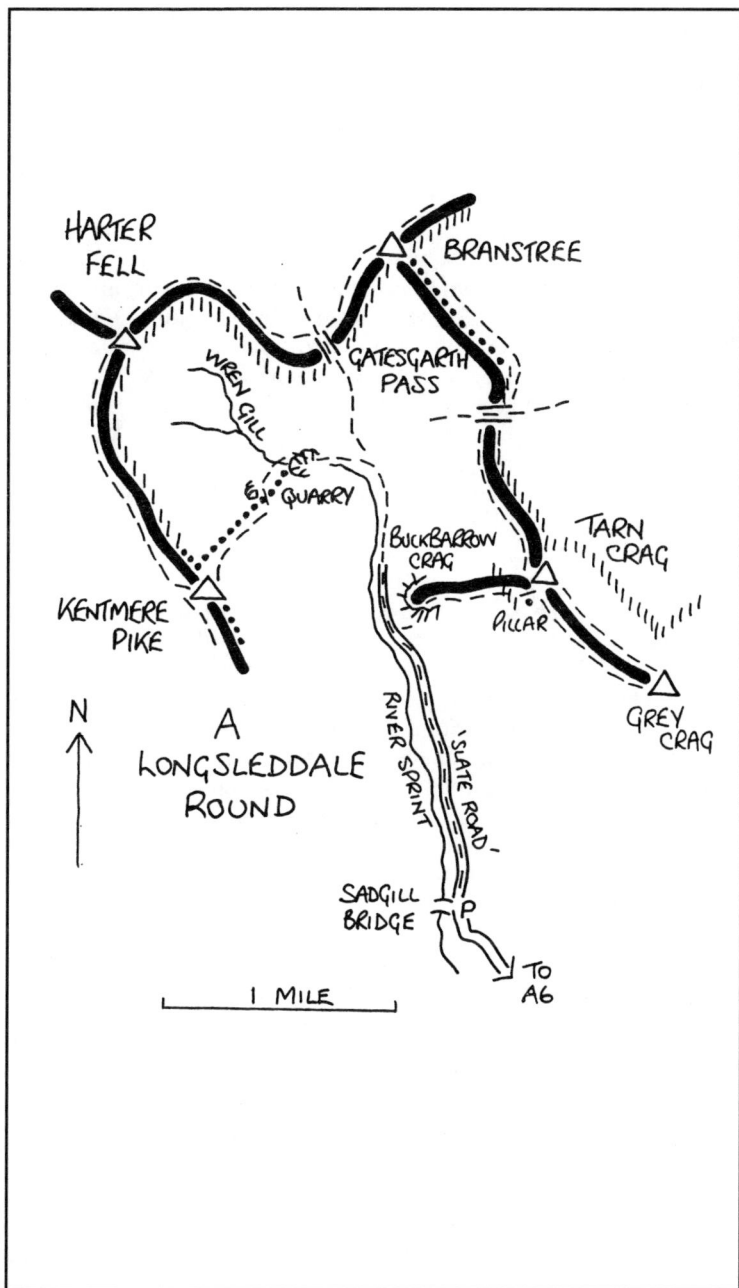

HARTER FELL

BRANSTREE

GATESGARTH PASS

WREN GILL

QUARRY

BUCKBARROW CRAG

TARN CRAG

KENTMERE PIKE

PILLAR

GREY CRAG

N

A LONGSLEDDALE ROUND

RIVER SPRINT

SLATE ROAD

SADGILL BRIDGE

P

TO A6

1 MILE

Branstree, 2339 feet. The tiny summit cairn stands a few paces beyond and gives a fine view of the rugged eastern ramparts and combes of High Street. From Branstree follow the fence south-west, down on to the saddle of Gatesgarth Pass.

Now climb the well-worn path that cuts a corner to rejoin the fence again on the south-east ridge of Harter Fell and continues alongside it to the summit. En route there are splendid 'birds-eye' views over the Haweswater Reservoir, marred, I feel, by the unnatural 'beach'. In the boiling summer of '84 the rapidly retreating water revealed the pathetic ruins of the drowned village of Mardale and brought traffic jams and ice-cream vendors to this normally tranquil valley. Harter Fell, 2552 feet, is crowned by a cairn incorporating rusty remnants of the old boundary fence. When fronded with ice it looks like a stand of surrealist weapons. North-westerly, Blea Water, Lakeland's deepest tarn, peers gloomily around a craggy corner of Mardale Ill Bell. (See Walk 2 for distant views.)

Now descend, initially south-south-westerly, alongside the fence, later wall, before climbing on to the summit of Kentmere Pike, 2394 feet. Climb over the wall, slap the trig-point, and walk left to a north-easterly heading wall and follow it valleywards. Some distance down, climb over the wall to explore a disused quarry/cave. Continue down between the wall and a beck to its confluence with Wren Gill. Cross the gill and follow a path down the far bank into the extensive ruins of Wren Gill Quarry. The water cascades into a boulder-choked pit and disappears underground before being regurgitated into the daylight lower down the quarry. It's thought that this quarry is the one referred to in a document of Edward I's reign which contains the earliest recorded reference to Lakeland quarrying. Continue through the quarry to a stile straddling a wall. Cross the stile and turn right to reach a gate leading on to the 'slate' road. Follow this down to your car.

# HIGH STREET (EAST)

**Walk 4**

**10 miles**
**2000 feet of ascent**

## Branstree, Selside Pike and the Old Corpse Road via Swindale & Mosedale Cottage

*A relatively easy walk that explores two of the more isolated upland valleys of eastern Lakeland and their enfolding fells. A walk of contrasts, wooded and cascaded Swindale leading into bleak and boggy Mosedale with its disused quarries and lonely bothy.*

*Parking: From Shap take the 'Haweswater' road. Fork left down through Rosgill, cross the River Lowther, and bear right to where a road forks sharply left, signposted 'Swindale 3 miles'. Follow this unfenced road to descend past a handsome stone Filter House to where the public road ends near a 'No Parking Beyond This Point' sign. Park here. (GR 522142).*

FOLLOW the road through pleasant woods, with the impressive buttresses of Gouther Crag towering across the valley, to where the tarmac ends near Swindale Head Farm. Beyond a gate a signpost indicates 'The Old Corpse Road' to your right and 'Mosedale' straight ahead. Continue up the valley to pass to the left of the swampy hollow of Dodd Bottom. Splitting the steep fellside beyond is the dark rift of Hobgrumble Gill, a succession of fine cascades gleaming in its shadowy depths.

When the path begins to climb steeply left, towards a marker pole on the skyline above, leave it. Descend left to the foot of the cascades of Mosedale Force. Scramble up the rocks and grass of the right bank of the Force, keeping as close to the water as possible. I think the final cascade the loveliest.

Above this fall the character of the terrain changes abruptly and you are entering bleaker Mosedale. A faint path bears right, away from the beck, to rejoin the bridleway where it runs alongside an old wall. Turn left along this somewhat boggy path. A hallmark of all Lakeland's 'mossy dales' is stretches of ankle-deep viscosity. On our last visit great dollops of frog spawn splattered the bogs, one of which I mistook for a stepping-stone and subsequently sank with all hands. The path climbs gradually right into Mosedale, passing several

17

marker posts. After passing above the footbridge carrying the Wet Sleddale-Mosedale path over Mosedale Beck, move left to join this somewhat firmer path. Turn right and follow this path through a gate in a fence to see before you Mosedale Cottage and its sheltering plantation. Mosedale saves a watery surprise for you, a beck to be crossed in order to reach the cottage. Should it be in spate you'll be very lucky to cross dryshod.

A section of the derelict building has been converted into a mountain bothy. The foul language in the 'logbook' and the wooden bunks smashed up for firewood make one question the value of bothies in Lakeland if they attract unwanted visitors who are obviously blind to the beauty and tranquillity around them and ignorant of its value in their lives.

As an aspiring bird watcher, I've found the environs of the cottage particularly rewarding. I've spotted kestrels, peregrines, buzzards and, once, one of Lakeland's golden eagles and, for a bonus, deer browsing on the flanks of Tarn Crag across the valley.

Cross Great Grain Gill behind the cottage and climb its right bank, passing some delightful cascades, into a grassy hollow where the gill forks. Cross near the fork and climb up the grassy tongue beyond, bearing gradually left, to meet a wall. As you climb, Longsleddale spreads away, below and behind your left shoulder, towards the Kent Estuary and far Morecambe Bay. Turn right and climb alongside the wall to a junction with a fence on the grassy dome of Branstree, 2339 feet. The summit lies a few yards beyond the fence. To the west and north-west the grassy whalebacks of Harter Fell, Mardale Ill Bell and High Street plunge precipitously into shadowy combes cupping the lovely upland tarns of Small Water and Blea Water.

Follow the fence north-east, passing close to the handsome cairn crowning Artle Crag. In the dip beyond cross the fence and walk easterly, passing a stone pillar that was used as a survey post during the construction of the Haweswater Reservoir and two small unnamed tarns, to reach the cairn crowning the unnamed and somewhat undistinguished peak beyond. At 2207 feet it is a must for all peak-baggers.

Head north to rejoin the fence again in the swampy dip below Selside Pike known as Captain Whelter Bog. Was the gallant captain a foxhunter who went down with all hounds here (ouch)? On several occasions I've spotted deer in the grassy western combe below. Climb alongside the fence to the cairn and stony wind shelter crowning Selside Pike, 2148 feet. Leave the fence corner and head north-north-east down a grassy ridge on to the broad boggy saddle crossed by the Old Corpse Road. Prior to 1736 the Mardale dead, strapped to sled or pony, were hauled over this path for burial in

Shap. Ironically, the bones of their descendants were disinterred and transported to Shap for burial when the valley was flooded.

Turn right along the path, which becomes more pronounced as it begins to descend into Swindale. The rocky bed of a gill is crossed and the path slants leftwards down the fellside towards a gate in the wall. Ignore this gate and descend alongside the wall to a gate leading into a muddy walled lane. Follow this down to Swindale Head Farm and a junction with your outward route.

*(See map on pages 24–25).*

**Walk 5**

**16 miles**
**4000 feet of ascent**

# A Haweswater Horseshoe

*A fine high level walk, not particularly strenuous despite its length, which for interest and enjoyment equals many of the more renowned 'horseshoes'.*

*Parking: From Shap, take the road to Haweswater. Just after passing the Burnbanks turnoff, crossing Naddle Bridge and passing the entrance to a private Water Board road, the road to Naddle Farm is reached. Park on the verges hereabouts. (GR 509157).*

WALK up the road to the farm. Go through the farmyard and a gate in the top left-hand corner. Cross Naddle Beck by a ford and climb a wooded path. Leave the wood and bear gradually right to another gate. Pass through this on to a crossing path. Turn right and follow this path, alongside a wall, to a gate in a dip. Beyond this gate leave the path and slant up on to the crest of the hills on your left. Beyond Hare Shaw, the high point of this group of undistinguished hillocks, head south-westerly to reach and cross the Old Corpse Road (see Walk 4) near the guidepost marking its highest point. (The cascades of Mosedale Beck, a feature of Walk 4, may be glimpsed down to your left.)

Now climb the grassy north-east ridge of Selside Pike, 2148 feet, to its stony summit wind shelter near a fence corner. Follow the fence just west-of-south down into a squelchy dip grandiosely named Captain Whelter Bog. The fence leads ultimately on to the summit of Branstree, passing between a crumbling stone survey pillar used in the construction of the Haweswater Reservoir and the handsome cairn crowning Artle Crag. It by-passes, however, an unnamed, and to be honest, undistinguished 2207 foot summit. Nevertheless, proper peakbaggers should make the diversion across the fence and back in order to capture this peak. You may spot deer in the big combe to your right.

From Branstree, 2339 feet, follow the fence south-westerly down on to the grassy saddle of Gatesgarth Pass. Climb the far slope up the path, cutting a corner to meet the fence again and continuing alongside it to the summit of Harter Fell. As you climb there's a fine view of Haweswater to your right. Harter Fell, 2552 feet, is crowned by a 'sculpture' of drystone and rusting ironwork. (See Walks 2 and 3 for brief descriptions of views).

Descend west, then north-westerly, down a stepped and rocky ridge, into the notch of Nan Bield Pass. With Kentmere Reservoir and volcano-like Ill Bell on the one hand, and Small Water and Haweswater on the other, it's a fine viewpoint; oftimes, however, a chilly wind-tunnel, its handsome shelter jammed with shivering walkers.

A good path climbs the rocky far slope to the cairn crowning Mardale Ill Bell, 2493 feet. Looming ahead now, like a giant whale with a knobbly backbone, is High Street and its crowning wall. A path dips before climbing north-westerly up easy grass to reach the wall near a cairn some distance south of the High Street trig-point. (Given 'white-out' conditions, it would be wise to take a compass bearing from Mardale Ill Bell, for these apparently amiable grasslands fall away precipitously on either hand).

Turn right and follow the wall up to the trig-point crowning High Street, 2716 feet. High Street takes its name from the Roman military road whose line crosses the dome to the west of the summit. The name Racecourse Hill on some maps stems from a time when shepherds used to meet here to exchange strays. This was as much a social as a business gathering and we are led to believe that horse racing, wrestling, and other appropriate Cumbrian junketting went on.

In mist, follow the wall north and down to the saddle named the Straits of Riggindale. Given clear weather, walk north-easterly on to the fell rim for views down on to Blea Water, Lakeland's deepest tarn, and Riggindale, the home of Lakeland's golden eagles, and follow the fell rim down to the Straits.

Climb up the far slope to where a cairn marks a path forking right. Turn right and follow this along the rim of Riggindale (you are now on the Roman Road) to a cluster of rocks. An ancient indecipherable guidepost may be spotted to your right. The 'Roman Road' now veers north-north-easterly, skirting the summit of Rampsgill Head and dropping on to the saddle below High Raise. You head north to 'bag' Rampsgill Head, 2598 feet. Walk beyond the tiny cairn for a dramatic view of rock towers rising against the green strath of Martindale, with the gleam of Ullswater beyond. Descend north-easterly on to a grassy saddle to pick up the Roman Road again and climb it on to the rock-scattered summit of High Raise, 2631 feet.

Around 6 a.m. one June morning, after we'd climbed High Street to see the sunrise, we were standing on High Raise when the silence was rudely broken by the roar of a motorbike. Suddenly, an ancient bike, driven by a be-goggled figure wearing a dated long leather coat and a leather ear-flapped hat, weaved and rattled across the summit and bounced away in the general direction of Penrith. He looked like a character out of 'Dawn Patrol', the classic film of aerial warfare in the First World War. It's my belief he was the ghost of a Roman despatch rider!!

From High Raise head east-north-easterly along a broad grassy spur to the cairn crowning Low Raise. Marked as a site of antiquity on the map, the sizeable cairn and neighbouring enclosure set amongst bare grasslands suggest the stones were manhandled some distance. For what purpose? Walk beyond the cairn to the rim of Whelter Crags. Follow the rim north around the huge Whelter Bottom combe and continue along the gradually descending fell rim overlooking Haweswater until a survey pillar is reached above Lad Crags. Now walk left around the fellside to find the start of an old sunken path that zig-zags down the steep slope of Measand End to reach a footbridge spanning Measand Beck. Don't cross the bridge. Turn right and follow the beck, passing above an impressive ravine and a succession of fine waterfalls, to reach the lakeshore path.

Glance up the glimmering lake at the now distant dalehead fells (have we walked that far?) before turning left across the bridge over the beck. Just over a mile later a stile, with a gate to its left, leads you down through the trees into the hamlet of Burnbanks. Turn left out of Burnbanks, looking for a 'Coast-to-Coast Walk' sign near a kissing gate on your right. Go through the gate and follow a path through woods to emerge on to the road near Naddle Bridge.

*(See map on pages 24–25).*

**11 miles
2500 feet of ascent**

# High Raise, Rampsgill Head and Kidsty Pike via Measand Beck

*This is a walk for those who like a sense of exploration, of remoteness, which can be found even in an ever crowded Lakeland, with a good chance of spotting deer, wild ponies, eagle and peregrine en route and ending with a visit to an eyrie of an ancient stronghold.*

*Parking: as for Walk 5.*

WALK back over Naddle Bridge, climb over the railings and down the steps on to a path signposted 'Burnbanks'. Follow it to a road and follow this into Burnbanks. Climb right from a 'Lakeshore Path' sign into woods where a further sign leads to a stile on the edge of the wood. Cross it and walk left along the rough track for about a mile to the gated footbridge spanning the Measand Beck. Don't cross the bridge. Walk back a few yards and climb the fellside, keeping as close as possible to the beck to enjoy the succession of splendid cascades (The Forces) surmounted by an impressive ravine. Above this the angle eases and a footbridge is reached. Ignore this and keep to the right bank of the beck which now serpentines through the swampy bowl of Fordingale Bottom. Keep to the firmer ground at the foot of the steep brackeny fellside to your right. Scrutinise this sun-facing fellside carefully and I can almost guarantee that you will spot deer browsing there.

Beyond Fordingale Bottom the flanks close in and you must scramble across the face of broken Force Crag, above the fine cascades of Fordingale Force, into the narrowing ravine beyond. Climb alongside the beck which eventually bears left to another fine waterfall. Above this the beck cascades through a rocky channel and you may find yourself forced on to the bouldery slopes to your right.

Beyond a confluence the beck swings right, the banks fall away, and you descend slightly into the hollow containing the confluence with the feeder becks of Longgrain and Keasgill Sike. Cross the Measand Beck below the confluence and climb left (south) up grassy slopes. Look out for deer and wild ponies hereabouts. Eventually you will emerge on to the airy rim of the huge Whelter Bottom combe, with Haweswater gleaming below. Climb right along the rim to its highest point, before veering right to the ancient cairn and enclosure crowning Low Raise. Walk west-south-westerly along a broad grassy ridge which steepens up on to the rock-strewn summit of High Raise, 2631 feet.

Walk west to join the 'Roman Road' and turn left down to the saddle below Rampsgill Head. At a fork turn right to 'bag' this 2598 foot peak. Walk to its northern rim for a peek down on to weathered rock pinnacles and a glimpse of Ullswater beyond the long dappled dale of Saint Martin.

Walk south across broad grasslands to the rim of Riggindale and a fine prospect of the High Street dome and its spiny ridges tumbling into Mardale. Walk left along the rim up onto the airy perch of Kidsty Pike, 2526 feet, a handy spot on a warm summer day to sit with binoculars and scour Riggindale for eagles and deer.

From Kidsty Pike head north-easterly down grassy slopes to reach the Randale Beck. Follow it down either bank, passing a sizeable sheepfold on the left bank, then a succession of small but lovely cascades. If you have not already done so, cross the beck to a lower sheepfold at the 'Ford' (GR 466125) marked on the 2½" map.

Follow a faint path (sheeptrod?) climbing leftwards and work your way around the fellside to Castle Crag. This is a grassy conical summit, guarded by a wall and crowned by a cairn and a decrepit iron fence, at the northern and lower end of a line of crags overlooking Haweswater and the shore path. It's the site of an 'Ancient Brit' stronghold. Cragged on three sides and guarded on the 'landward' side by what appears to be a double ditch, it is eminently defensible, probably only used as a place of refuge when danger threatened. The views up and down the reservoir are superb, but we must remind ourselves that it is not what our ancestors would have seen.

Descend back to the wall and follow it right, along the ditch, to pick up a path which zig-zags steeply down into Whelter Bottom. Go to the right of an isolated plantation to join the lakeshore path and follow it left to a junction with your outward route at the footbridge spanning Measand Beck.

Given bad weather conditions, an easier alternative from Kidsty Pike would be to follow the worn path down the east ridge, over the rocky humps of Kidsty Howes, and down into Riggindale. Don't cross the wooden footbridge over the Riggindale Beck. Turn left over the handsome stone packhorse bridge spanning the Randale Beck and return along the lakeshore path to a junction with your outward route at the Measand Beck.

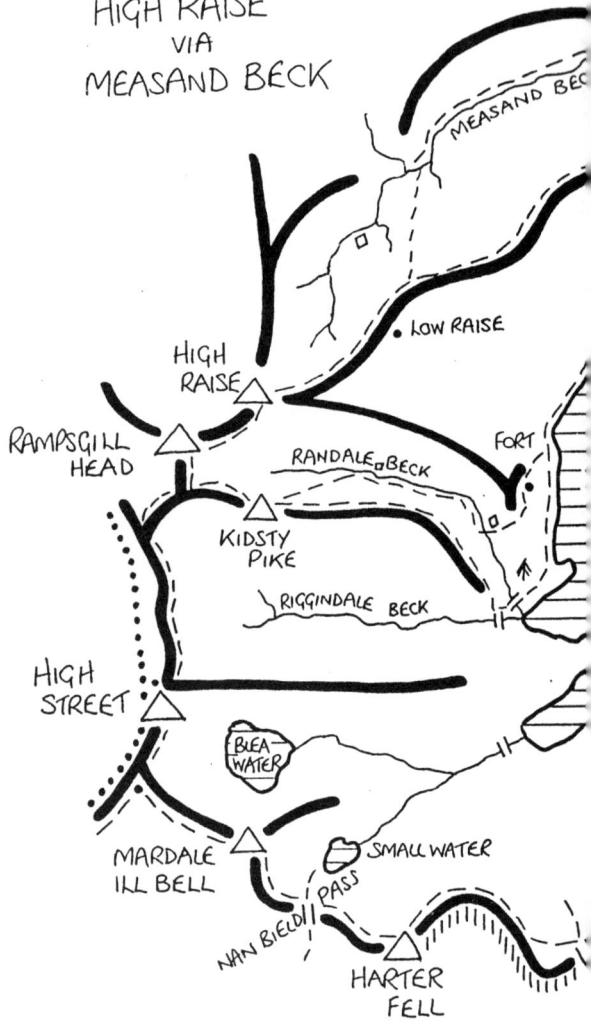

# HIGH RAISE
## VIA
## MEASAND BECK

MEASAND BECK

LOW RAISE

HIGH
RAISE

RAMPSGILL
HEAD

RANDALE BECK

FORT

KIDSTY
PIKE

RIGGINDALE BECK

HIGH
STREET

BLEA-
WATER

MARDALE
ILL BELL

SMALLWATER

NAN BIELD PASS

HARTER
FELL

## A HAWESWATER
## HORSESHOE

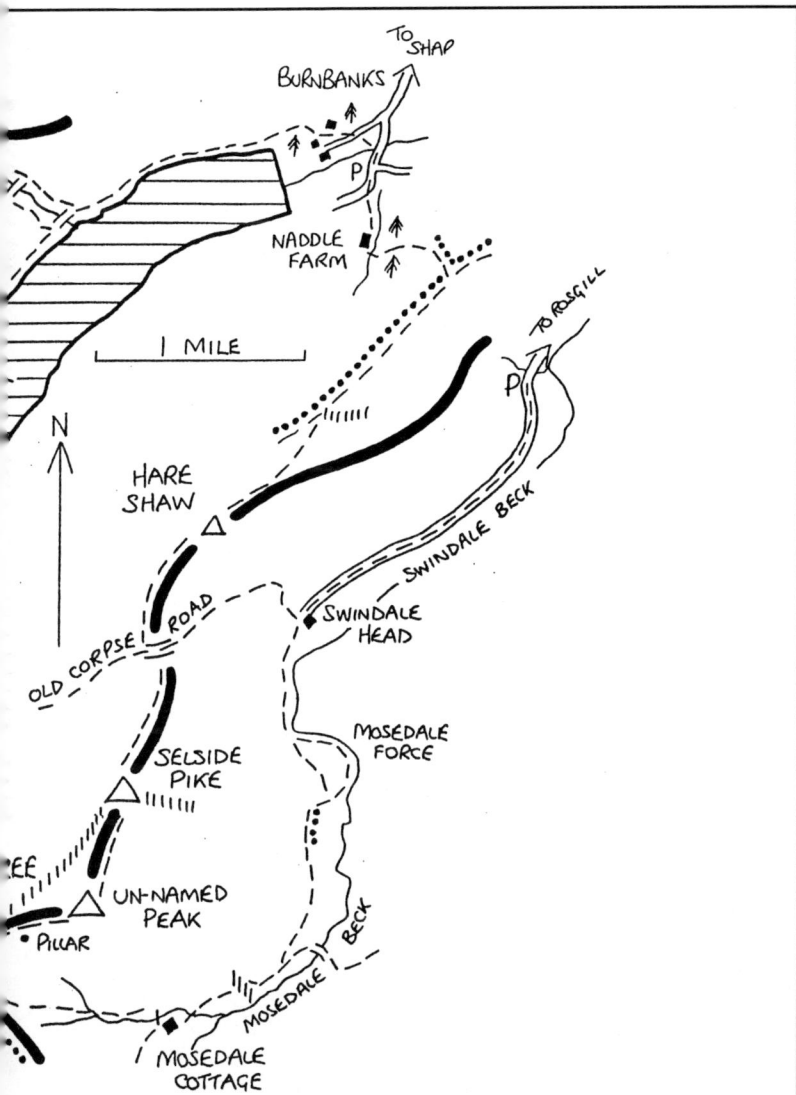

TO SHAP

BURNBANKS

P

NADDLE
FARM

1 MILE

N

HARE
SHAW

TO ROSGILL

P

SWINDALE BECK

OLD CORPSE ROAD

SWINDALE
HEAD

MOSEDALE
FORCE

SELSIDE
PIKE

EE

UN-NAMED
PEAK

PILLAR

MOSEDALE BECK

MOSEDALE
COTTAGE

BRANSTREE AND SELSIDE PIKE
VIA SWINDALE

**Walk 7**                    9 miles – 2800 feet of ascent
                        or 12 miles – 3500 feet of ascent

# The Mardale Skyline

*The head of Mardale is encircled by grassy, whaleback fells, though a stranger looking up from the carpark at the head of Haweswater would find this hard to believe. For around him thrusts rock, the greeny crags of Harter Fell riven by dank gullies, the scree fans and piled boulders of Rough Crag, and yet more rock spilling over the distant skyline of High Street and Mardale Ill Bell. The walk described below takes you around the high rim of this rugged dalehead.*

*Parking: The carpark at the head of Haweswater (GR 469108).*

GO through the gate beyond the carpark to shortly reach a signpost by a wall corner. Turn right and follow the 'Public Footpath to Bampton' down to a footbridge over the Mardale Beck. Cross the bridge, turn right, and follow the path that eventually climbs leftwards towards the crest of The Rigg, the wooded promontory dividing the headwaters of Haweswater. Just before reaching the crest a path forks left. Ignore this and continue over the crest of the spur through a gap in a wall to the left of a plantation.

Walk down the far slope into Riggindale and towards a copse. Should the reservoir be low a complex of old walls, lanes and tumbled buildings will be displayed on the muddy shore of the bay to your right. Sizeable convoys of Canada Geese may also be spotted offshore, or disembarking en masse upon it. For many years now Riggindale has been the home of Lakeland's solitary pair of Golden Eagles. During the nesting season voluntary wardens from the R.S.P.B. maintain a watch over the nest but welcome visitors to view it from their 'hide' a few hundred yards upstream from the copse.

Go through the copse and along the stone-lined path beyond to a footbridge over the Riggindale Beck. Cross this and climb up the fellside ahead, to ultimately emerge on to the east ridge of Kidsty Pike through the rocky outcrops of Kidsty Howes. Now climb gradually westwards towards the graceful cone of Kidsty Pike, 2562 feet. The summit cairn is perched on the airy rim of a slabby crag, a fine vantage point of your prospective expedition or should the eagles take wing. Now you will see that all that macho mountain swagger viewed from the carpark was all bluff and bluster and you'll spend most of the day walking on grass. Good high-level stuff though, with exciting prospects all around.

Continue following the fell rim westwards onto a section of the 'Roman Road' (see Walk 13), before swinging left to join a path and wall dropping left on to the high saddle called Straits of Riggindale. Across Riggindale looms the massive dome of High Street. Mark the path climbing rightwards from the Straits and around its western shoulder. This is the line of the 'Roman Road'.

Climb out of the Straits, keeping to the left side of the wall. When the angle eases and the wall veers south on to the summit leave it and walk left along the fell rim to a cairn marking the exit from Long Stile (see Walk 8). Step to the edge for an eagle's view of Blea Water, Lakeland's dark and deepest tarn, and the rugged combes and ridges tumbling down into flooded Mardale. Walk back to the wall and follow it leftwards to reach the trig-point crowning High Street, 2716 feet. (See Walks 5 and 13 for historical notes).

Leave the trig-point and head south, keeping to the left of the wall. Far ahead, Windermere weaves a gleaming highway, traffic-jammed with islands, through darkly wooded foothills. Ranked closer are Yoke, Ill Bell and Froswick, the cream of the Kentmere Horseshoe. Keep your eyes open for a cairn to the left of the wall marking the start of a path forking left.

Now follow the description in Walk 2 from "Turn left here to descend south-easterly over broad grasslands" to "high jumble of the Scafells to its left".

Now follow the fence, and its sidekick path, initially north-east, but ultimately and easily down on to the grassy saddle of Gatesgarth Pass, revelling en route in the fine views of Haweswater. One winter we descended this way to find meltwater had turned lower sections of the path into treacherous mud slides. Suddenly a girl in front of us went sprawling on her back. A few yards further and 'SPLAT', down she went again. As she painfully arose, dripping with goo, her male companion spoke to her. Obviously his remark was uncomplimentary, for she dealt him a vicious right hook and 'SPLURT', down he went! We sidled past them, she in tears and he a picture of confused male pride, virtually rupturing ourselves with bottled up laughter.

Turn left on Gatesgarth Pass, and a good path leads you down to the carpark. Should the day be young and you're feeling fit enough for three more modest two-thousanders, climb up the far slope alongside the fence on to the summit of Branstree, 2339 feet. Now follow the description given in Walk 4 from "Follow the fence north-east, passing close to the handsome cairn crowning Artle Crag" to "valley was flooded". Now turn left along the Corpse Road, which improves as it steepens down into Mardale above the ravine of Rowantreethwaite Beck. From hereabouts, look across the gleaming headwaters of Haweswater at the long and lumpy skyline you have traversed and give yourself a deserved pat on the back. A gate leads on to the road. Cross it to a gate signposted 'Public Footpath/Head of the Lake'. Follow this pleasant lakeshore path back to the carpark.

**Walk 8**    **Variation A: 7 miles – 2500 feet of ascent**
**or 10 miles – 3200 feet of ascent**
**Variation B: 7 miles – 2200 feet of ascent**

# High Street via Rough Crag and Long Stile

*For the fellwalker this ridge is probably the most exciting way of climbing High Street. Though not as narrow or airy as the more glamorous 'edges', such as Sharp, Striding or Swirrel, it is enjoyable throughout with most of the excitement coming as you approach the summit, which is as it should be. When coated in snow or ice, however, Long Stile can become a serious proposition and should not be attempted without the proper equipment, e.g. ice axe and crampons.*

*Parking/Start: As for Walk 7.*

FOLLOW the description in Walk 7 as far as "just before reaching the crest a path forks left".

Fork left along this path to shortly climb alongside the wall that crowns the crest of the ridge. An initial steep climb eventually eases on to a well-defined ridge falling steeply away on either hand. The wall turns down into Riggindale shortly before you reach the summit of Rough Crag. Rough Crag, 2060 feet, is an added bonus for the peak-bagger, and a good spot for a breather and a session of 'eagle-spotting' over Riggindale. Below, to your left, lies the vast, crag-lined hollow cupping Blea Water, the 'black water'. I have swum in many of the high tarns but never in this sombre water, which has been plumbed to a depth of over two hundred feet. The thought of swimming over that gives me goose pimples! The high corries, especially those graced by a tarn, be they mailed in ice or brimful of sunlight and the dazzle-flicker of water, are truly and breathtakingly the 'cathedrals of the mountains'.

Beyond Rough Crag the ridge dips on to the grassy saddle of Caspel Gate, crowned by its tiny, unnamed tarn. Long Stile's steep and rocky stairway leads out of Caspel Gate. The path twists and

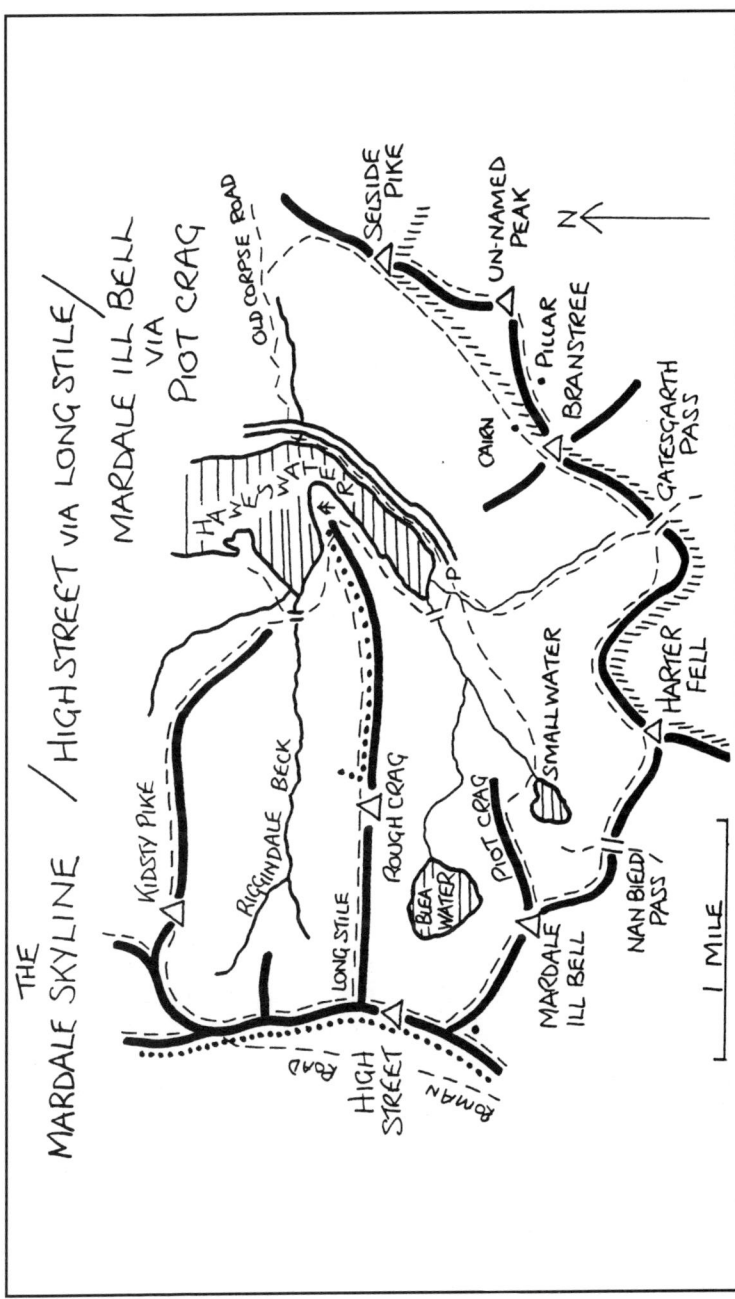

THE
MARDALE SKYLINE / HIGH STREET VIA LONG STILE /
MARDALE ILL BELL
VIA
PIOT CRAG

SELSIDE PIKE
UN-NAMED PEAK
OLD CORPSE ROAD
PILLAR
BRANSTREE
CAIRN
GATESGARTH PASS
HARVEST WATER
P
HARTER FELL
KIDSTY PIKE
RIGGINDALE BECK
ROUGH CRAG
SMALLWATER
PIOT CRAG
LONG STILE
BLEA WATER
MARDALE ILL BELL
NAN BIELD PASS /
HIGH STREET
ROMAN ROAD
N
1 MILE

29

climbs around the rocky hummocks, giving, under normal conditions, a straightforward climb enlivened by an all round sense of depth and space. It must be obvious, however, that a slip here, given the fell was coated in hard snow or ice, could have serious consequences. Should these conditions pertain, come prepared.

Step on to the grassy summit dome and walk south-west to shortly reach the trig-point and wall crowning High Street, 2716 feet. High Street takes its name from the Roman military road linking the forts sited at Penrith and Ambleside, which crosses the fell about a hundred yards west of the summit. (See Walks 5 and 13 for historical notes). The prospect from High Street is wide-ranging but distant (a visitor in 1821 wrote that it embraced 'the Scotch Mountains'), everything close at hand being hidden by the spread of the summit dome. It is from the rims, looking down on to Blea Water or Haweswater, that the most dramatic views are seen.

From High Street, at least two options, other than a return down Long Stile, are open to you:

Variation A: You could now follow the description given in Walk 7 over Mardale Ill Bell and Harter Fell, etc., and so down to the valley, or

Variation B: Reverse the first half of Walk 7 and return to the valley via the Straights of Riggindale and Kidsty Pike. Imaginative scrutiny of your map will possibly open your eyes to yet other interesting ways back to your car.

**Walk 9**     **Variation A; 5 miles – 2300 feet of ascent**
**or 8 miles – 3000 feet of ascent**
**Variation B: 7 miles – 2100 feet of ascent**

# Mardale Ill Bell via Small Water & Piot Crag

*Like the previous walk, this is a direct ascent on to the High Street massif, involving some easy scrambling. Unlike the Rough Crag/Long Stile ridge, however, this is an unfrequented route, which undoubtedly adds to its attractions.*

*Parking/Start: As for Walk 7.*

GO through the gate beyond the carpark to shortly reach a signpost near a wall corner. Follow the 'Public Bridleway to Kentmere' sign. This well-worn path slants gradually upwards under the green and grotty gullies and crags of Harter Fell. It steepens for the final climb up to Small Water, climbing virtually alongside the delightful cascades of Small Water Beck.

Stepping stones lead across the beck where it spills from the tarn. Small Water is a gem of a mountain tarn. Here rock and water, the quintessence of Lakeland fell scenery, are sublimely matched. Immediately after crossing the stepping stones, look up to your right where a succession of grassy or rock-tipped hillocks form the Piot Crag Ridge. Having paid due obesiance to the beauty of Small Water climb up the grassy bank to the right of the path, pass behind some large flattish boulders, and climb up steepish grass to the first dip in the ridge. Turn left here and it's simply a matter of picking what you feel is the most interesting line up the two rocky steps, each with an apron of bouldery scree at its foot, which rise ahead. Both can be skirted but it's more fun to climb them. The second crag offers more of a challenge.

On our last visit we climbed a groove on to a grass ledge. We then traversed left and slightly down along the ledge to reach the rocky rim of an obvious gully. We then climbed the clean rocks overlooking the gully, which gave an easy scramble in a fine situation. It's all a matter of picking a line to suit your nerve. On a scale of one to ten my nerve rates about three, on a good day, so anything I've described can be climbed in the wet by a Granny packing the ubiquitous kitchen sink.

Awaiting you, above this crag, are the decrepit workings of a quarry, something of a surprise at this height. A slabby wall to the right offers a bit of fun to the scrambler. Above the quarry the angle eases, the ridge broadens, and a steady plod upwards brings you slap-bang up against the summit cairn of Mardale Ill Bell, 2493 feet. On the way look for an unusual view of the windshelter crowning Nan Bield Pass and the rocky north-west ridge of Harter Fell.

From Mardale Ill Bell two options are open to you:

Variation A: You could now follow the description given in Walk 7 down to Nan Bield Pass and up over Harter Fell, etc.

Variation B: You could reverse Walk 7 back over High Street and Kidsty Pike.

# HIGH STREET (WEST)

**Walk 10**                                                    **11 miles**
**3500 feet of ascent**

# A Boredale Round

*An interesting and varied walk that feels harder when you've finished
than the figures would suggest. It involves two fairly long and unrelenting
climbs, which is probably the reason why. Don't let me put you off.
Having never walked it in its entirety I tested it on a 'dreich' squally day
of low cloud and chilly drizzle and was still impressed enough to feel
I had to include it in this guidebook. I'm looking forward to going back
on a good day. Perhaps I might meet you.*

*Parking: Cow Bridge. The carparks on either bank of the Goldrill
Beck on the A592 just north of Brotherswater, marked 'Cow Bridge'
on the North-East sheet of the 2½" maps. (GR 403134).*

WALK south-east along the A592 to the 'Hartsop' turnoff. Turn left
down this then almost immediately left behind a house into a walled
track. Follow this to a footbridge spanning Angletarn Beck. Cross
the bridge. Now climb steeply right up a path on the left bank of the
beck. Above some fine waterfalls the path slants towards the beck
under a steepening of the left bank. Cross the levellish beck and
climb up the far bank to a wall. Go through a gap in the wall and turn
left along a narrow path on its far side. Continue on to where beck,
path and wall squeeze, interestingly, through a rocky ravine before
the angle eases and boggy ground leads to the shore of Angle Tarn.

   Turn left through a gap in the wall, cross the beck, and follow a path
swinging right around a rocky hump guarding the shore. When past
the hump climb left up the fellside, crossing a well-worn path, and
head up to the right of some obvious rocks, a sheltered spot for a
'breather' and to gaze upon the tarn. Climb steeply alongside the
rocks to easier ground. Climb right around a hump guarded by a rock
finger to see the south 'pike' of Angle Tarn Pikes rising ahead. Both
have narrow crests and offer panoramic views over Brotherswater,
Kirkstone Pass and their enfolding fells. According to the map the
north 'pike' is the higher by two metres.

   From it head north-easterly, passing to the left of a swampy tarn,
towards a conical grassy hill, marked 550 metres on the 2½" map. Climb
over its right shoulder to find a path which quickly improves as it
leads on to the long, undulating ridge that divides Boredale from

Bannerdale and Martindale. Head north-easterly along this ridge, ignoring a crossing path below Beda Fell Knott. From the top of Beda Head there is an exciting view of the lower reaches of Ullswater. A long descent from Beda Head leads to a climb over the spiky summit rocks of Howstead Brow.

Down to your right is the old church of St. Martin. The original church was built in the thirteenth century and some of its stones survive in the present structure. The yew, whose choleric limbs crowd one corner of the churchyard, is reputedly seven hundred years old, and the font is thought to be part of a Roman altar. Here, the Reverend Birkett shepherded his flock through the traumatic years of the Civil Wars for a stipend of £6.13.4d. He must have been a formidably parsimonious cleric for he is reputed to have left £1,300, a fortune in those days!

Beyond Howstead Brow a path drops left on to the Boredale road near Garth Head Farm. (Slanting leftwards up the fellside above the farm is the path you will shortly climb on to Place Fell. It's a good idea, from here, to work out which lower path connects with it.). Cross the road and a stile to the right of the farm then walk left to a clapper-bridge (slate/stone slab spanning a beck) over the Boredale Beck. Cross this and climb left, past a 'Permitted Footpath' sign, to a gate. Beyond the gate, climb right alongside a wall. Fork left and climb up to the higher path slanting left across the fellside. Plod steadily up this to where it twists steeply right to join a crossing path.

Climb left along this and shortly the angle eases and you emerge on to the grassy saddle of Low Moss. Pass to the left of a sheepfold and climb the well-worn path that leads you to the trig-point crowning the rocky tor that's the summit of Place Fell, 2155 feet. Spread before you, if you're lucky, are the rugged coves, spiny ridges and green drumlin-dimpled dales that are the joy of the Fairfield–Helvellyn massif.

Descend south, along the rim of the fell, climb over the subsidiary summit of Round How, descend the shaly gully beyond, and zig-zag down onto the grassy saddle of Boredale Hause.

Boredale Hause is a kind of mountain Piccadilly Circus with paths going off in all directions. To avoid confusion, face west, looking down into the Patterdale Valley, and take the path descending left. It shortly crosses a bouldery culvert channelling Stonebarrow Gill, a positive indicator that you are on the right path. Continue down to a crossing path where a left turn brings you to a junction with your outward route at the Angletarn Beck footbridge.

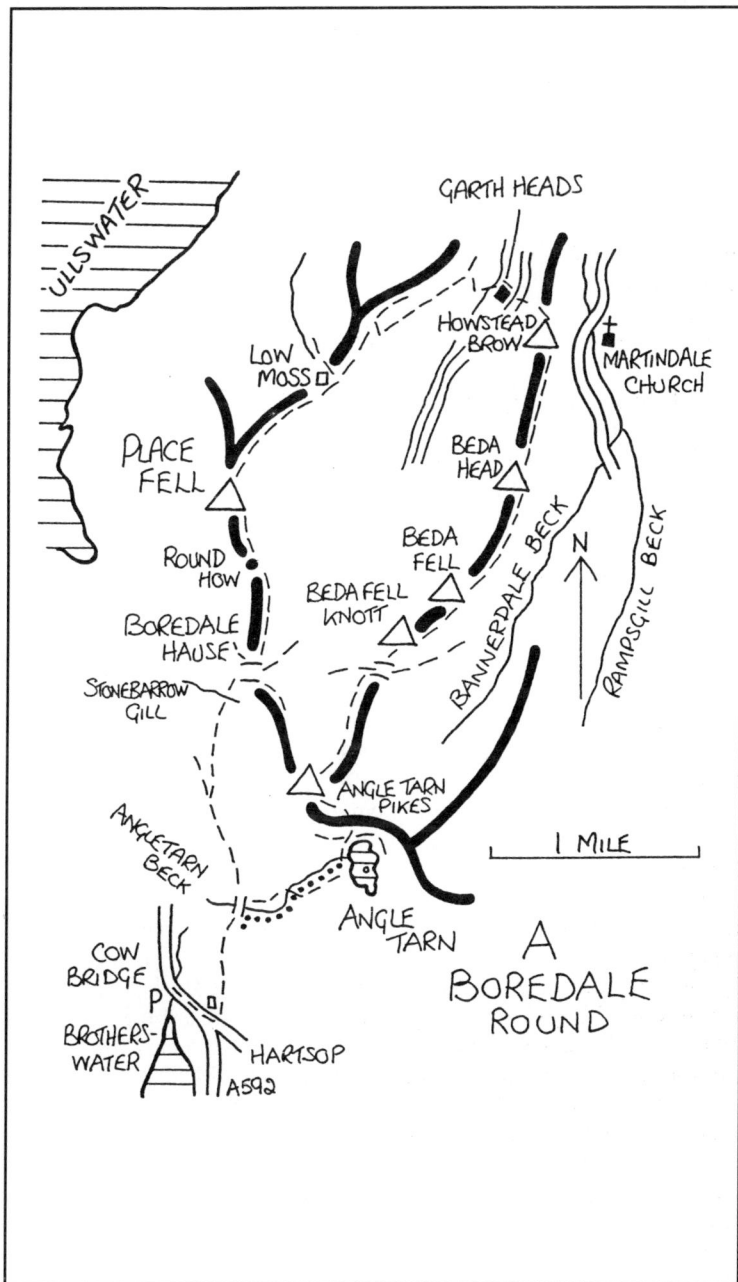

ULLSWATER

GARTH HEADS

LOW MOSS □

HOWSTEAD BROW △

MARTINDALE CHURCH ✝

PLACE FELL △

BEDA HEAD △

ROUND HOW

BEDA FELL △

BOREDALE HAUSE

BEDA FELL KNOTT △

BANNERDALE BECK

RAMPSGILL BECK

N ↑

STONEBARROW GILL

ANGLE TARN PIKES △

ANKLETARN BECK

1 MILE

COW BRIDGE

P

BROTHERS-WATER

ANGLE TARN

HARTSOP

A592

A BOREDALE ROUND

# The Hartsop Round

*An entertaining walk that involves a considerable amount of climbing and finishes with a descent that leaves your knees feeling as if they are made of warm blancmange. Good fun though. The views are varied and superb and it gives you a 'bag' of five two-thousand footers. A splendid day out.*

*Parking: The carpark at the Hartsop road end. (GR 409131).*

WALK back out of the carpark. Follow a 'Footpath' sign right, up to a gate. Climb a partially metalled drive before descending to the dwelling of 'Grey Rigg'. Follow a 'Patterdale' sign right through a narrow passageway, then along a path descending through woods to a stile in a wall corner. Cross the stile and Angletarn Beck beyond, then follow the description in Walk 10 from "Now climb steeply right up a path on the left bank of the beck" to "crossing a well-worn path".

Do not cross this path but instead turn right and follow it around the tarn. Angle Tarn is a lovely spot to pause for a 'breather', or even a dip, given the weather. Continue along the path, climbing above the eastern shore. If it's clear move left on to the grassy crest and follow rotting wood posts up on to the summit of Buck Crag, a splendid viewpoint over Bannerdale and Martindale. South-easterly, gloomy Hayeswater is set in its bare bowl of fells.

Drop south to rejoin the path where it passes through a gate in a wall. Continue alongside the wall/fence until the path turns right through a gap in it. Leave the path here and climb steeply leftwards, alongside the wall at first but gradually veering away from it to reach the grassy summit of Rest Dodd, 2283 feet, a relatively unfrequented peak overlooking Martindale. The red-roofed building in Martindale is The Bungalow. Formerly a hunting lodge of the Earls of Lonsdale, it was visited by Kaiser Wilhelm II shortly before the First World War. Scrutinise carefully the bare bowl of Upper Martindale, dominated by be-pinnacled Rampsgill Head, and you may spot deer.

Drop south to a wall corner and follow the wall south-easterly into a dip then up to rejoin your original path where it passes through a gap in the wall. Turn left along the path which climbs right into the gap between Rampsgill Head and Knott to meet a wall corner. (A short diversion right, up alongside the wall, and back, would 'bag' the summit of Knott, 2424 feet.) Beyond the gap path and wall drop on to the Straits of Riggindale saddle. Ahead looms the great dome of

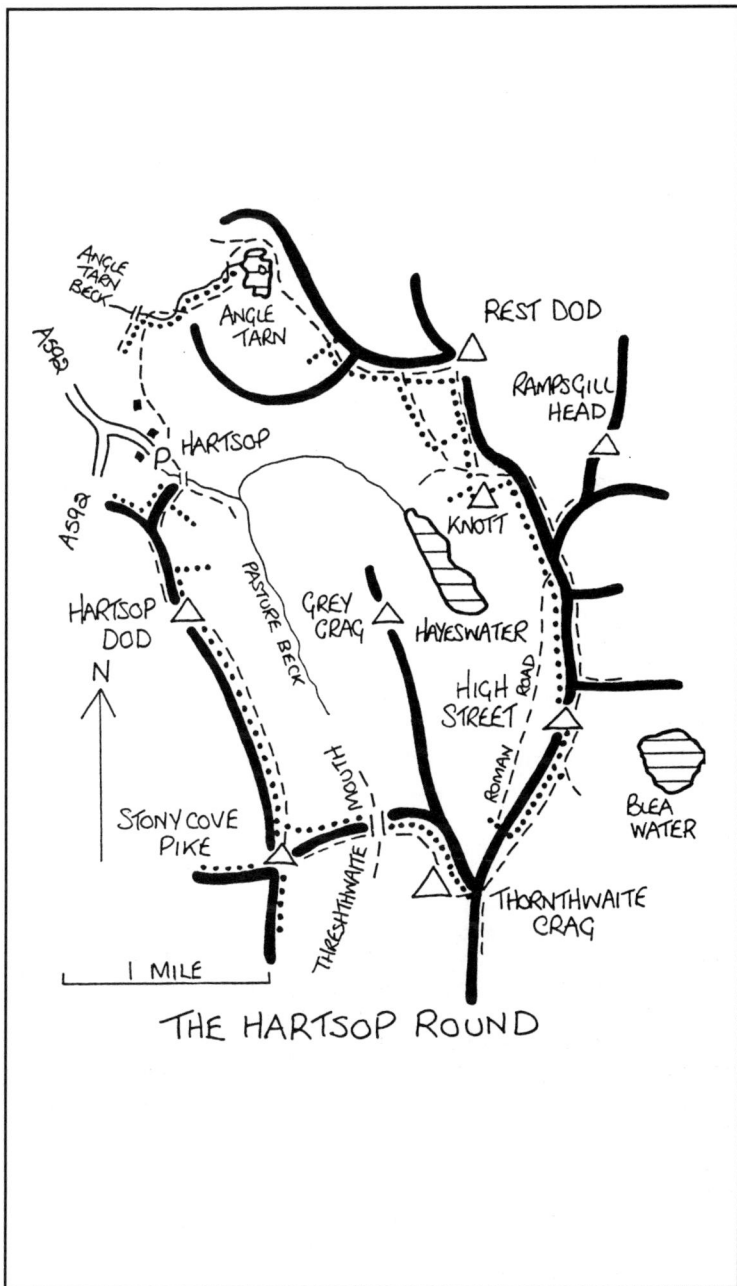

THE HARTSOP ROUND

Map labels:
- ANGLE TARN BECK
- ANGLE TARN
- REST DOD
- RAMPSGILL HEAD
- A592
- HARTSOP
- P
- KNOTT
- A592
- HARTSOP DOD
- N
- PASTURE BECK
- GREY CRAG
- HAYESWATER
- HIGH STREET
- ROMAN ROAD
- BLEA WATER
- STONY COVE PIKE
- THRESHTHWAITE MOUTH
- THORNTHWAITE CRAG
- 1 MILE

High Street, monarch of the eastern fells. Climb between the wall and the fell rim dropping precipitously into Riggindale. This is 'eagle country', so keep your eyes open. When the angle eases and the wall veers south, move left to a cairn on the fell rim. There is an excellent view of the Long Stile ridge, High Street's finest, which emerges here, and Blea Water (see Walk 2). Return to the wall and follow it up to the trig-point crowning High Street, 2716 feet.

Continue alongside the wall in a gradual descent. Ranked ahead are the shapely cones of Froswick, Ill Bell and Yoke, and beyond them the dazzle-flicker miles of Lakeland's longest lake. Beyond the wall corner take the path forking right in a south-west to west swing around the rim of the Hayeswater combe and on up to the summit of Thornthwaite Crag, 2572 feet. The chimney-like cairn is a work of art and an intrinsic and challenging feature in this complex of grassy cones and domes. Go through the gap in its supporting wall, turn right, and follow this wall down onto the saddle of Threshthwaite Mouth. The ground becomes steep and rough before the saddle is reached, and care should be taken in winter conditions.

Follow the wall across the saddle to the foot of the steep rocky east ridge of Stony Cove Pike. (At this point it's possible to 'escape' by going through a gap in the wall and following a path down into the valley of the Pasture Beck and subsequently on to Hartsop.)

If attacked with determination, the climb proves less painful than might be expected. In fact it's quite enjoyable, offering snippets of easy rock-scrambling. Eventually the angle eases, the rock submerges, and the path continues alongside a wall. Just before reaching a wall junction it veers left, south-west, to reach the cairn that appears to be accepted as the summit of Stony Cove Pike, 2503 feet, although there are other apparently equally high bumps scattered around.

Walk a short distance beyond the cairn to a wall. Turn right and walk alongside it to reach a wall corner. Climb over the crossing wall and continue with the original wall to your left. Follow the wall down a broad grassy ridge into the dip below Hartsop Dod, your final peak. The fellside beyond the wall slopes into the grassy bowl of Caudale. Crumbling workshops and fans of spoil green into the flank of this lonely mountain sanctuary which frequently shelters deer.

Follow the wall up on to the summit of Hartsop Dod, 2027 feet. Go through a gap in the wall to visit the cairn and continue, with the wall to your right, down the far slope. When the wall turns away, follow cairns down an ever-steepening path giving a truly 'birds-eye' view of Hartsop, the Vale of Patterdale and the head of Ullswater. Glance left into the heart of Dovedale, where the sinking sun may be highlighting the ancient 'standing stones' in the fields at the valley mouth.

At a wall corner fork right and follow the wall down to a gate. Continue steeply, and soggily hereabouts, trying not to splatter on to your 'bum', down to a bridge over the beck and wobble thankfully across it to journeys end.


**Walk 12**                                    **12 miles**
                                    **5000 feet of ascent**

# The Five Tarns Walk

*This is one for the fellwalker who loves a challenge, a round trip touching the shores of each of the five major tarns in the High Street massif, but be prepared for long rough climbs followed by equally long and rough descents. It's worth every drop of sweat, passing through some superb mountain scenery. It'll send the temperature in your knees up into the red, but at the end of the day you'll have earned every drop of that celebratory pint.*

*Parking: As for Walk 11.*

GO through the gate, pass the sheep-pens, and follow the path that passes above the fine cascades and rock pools of Hayeswater Gill to end at the Hayeswater Dam. Head to the right of the dam along a narrow path passing below the steep north-easterly flank of Grey Crag. Beyond the head of the reservoir follow the feeder beck and its companion wall through a barrier of handsome drumlins crowned here and there with massive boulders. Beyond, the valley walls close steeply in. The 'ambience' is that of a remote Scottish glen rather than a Lakeland valley. In dry weather the gill bed gives an entertaining scrambly stairway of slabby waterworn rock. Emerge, eventually, on to the worn path crossing the broad grassy saddle linking High Street and Thornthwaite Crag. (The latter's chimney-like cairn will be seen rising close to your right).

Turn left to the wall corner. Walk a short distance just east of south from the wall corner to find yourself on a path crossing the rim of a wide shaly gully. Slither down the gully and follow the emergent beck, the source of the River Kent, down into the lonely hollow of Hall Cove, passing a large sheepfold. From here Yoke, Ill Bell and Froswick do their utmost to emulate the Three Sisters of Glencoe. They don't make it, but it's a damned good try. Continue down alongside the infant Kent, right bank then left bank, around and under Lingmell End, to reach the wall enclosing Kentmere Reservoir.

Turn left where Lingmell Gill breaches this enclosing wall and climb alongside it into the grassy combe below Nan Bield Pass. Cross the gill and angle right to join the public bridleway linking Kentmere and Mardale over the Nan Bield. Climb its final steep zig-zags to reach the handsome shelter crowning the pass.

Descend the far slope down the steep path which eases out on to the western shore of Small Water. Note the drystone shelters which Mr. Wainwright suggests were built as 'bivvies' for travellers overtaken by darkness or bad weather in the days when this bridleway was principally used by traders or itinerant workers, not frivolous fellwalkers!

Beyond the 'shelters' the path curves around the tarn, climbing slightly. Leave it where it begins to climb and walk left into a grassy hollow between a vegetated crag (left) and a pointed slabby hillock. Go down and around the base of the small boulder field below the crag and up to a path climbing around the edge of the crag. This leads on to a crest overlooking a boggy combe. Blea Water lies hidden behind the ridge guarding the head of the combe. Make a descending traverse across the fellside to your left into the head of the combe. Turn right and cross the combe to reach the bank of Blea Water Beck. Cross the beck and climb the far bank to join a path which leads you up to the Blea Water Dam.

Climb north-westerly from the dam to arrive on to the popular Rough Crags/Long Stile ridge at the foot of the latter. Now grit your teeth for Long Stile's steep rocky hummocks. You may be a touch 'cream-crackered' by now and counting steps, a useful mantra when the pain barrier threatens.

From the cairn where Long Stile exits on to the High Street dome the trig-point lies a short climb south-westerly. 'Bag' it by all means, but it's not compulsory. This walk culls tarns not peaks, so you can happily walk north-westerly to reach the wall and follow it northwards down onto the Straits of Riggindale. Now, although you've still got 'miles to go before you sleep', they're largely downhill miles.

Follow the wall up the far slope to where it swings left on to the summit of Knott. You stay with the path which swings left, around Knott, and through a gap in a wall. When opposite a large slabby rock to your left crowned by a wall and a spike of fence, fork right. Hartsop is visible below but you must 'stiffen the sinews and summon up the blood' and turn away from it along this oftimes boggy path that slants down across the south-west flank of Rest Dod, then swings westerly over Satura Crag, before descending north-westerly to the shore of your final watery target, Angle Tarn.

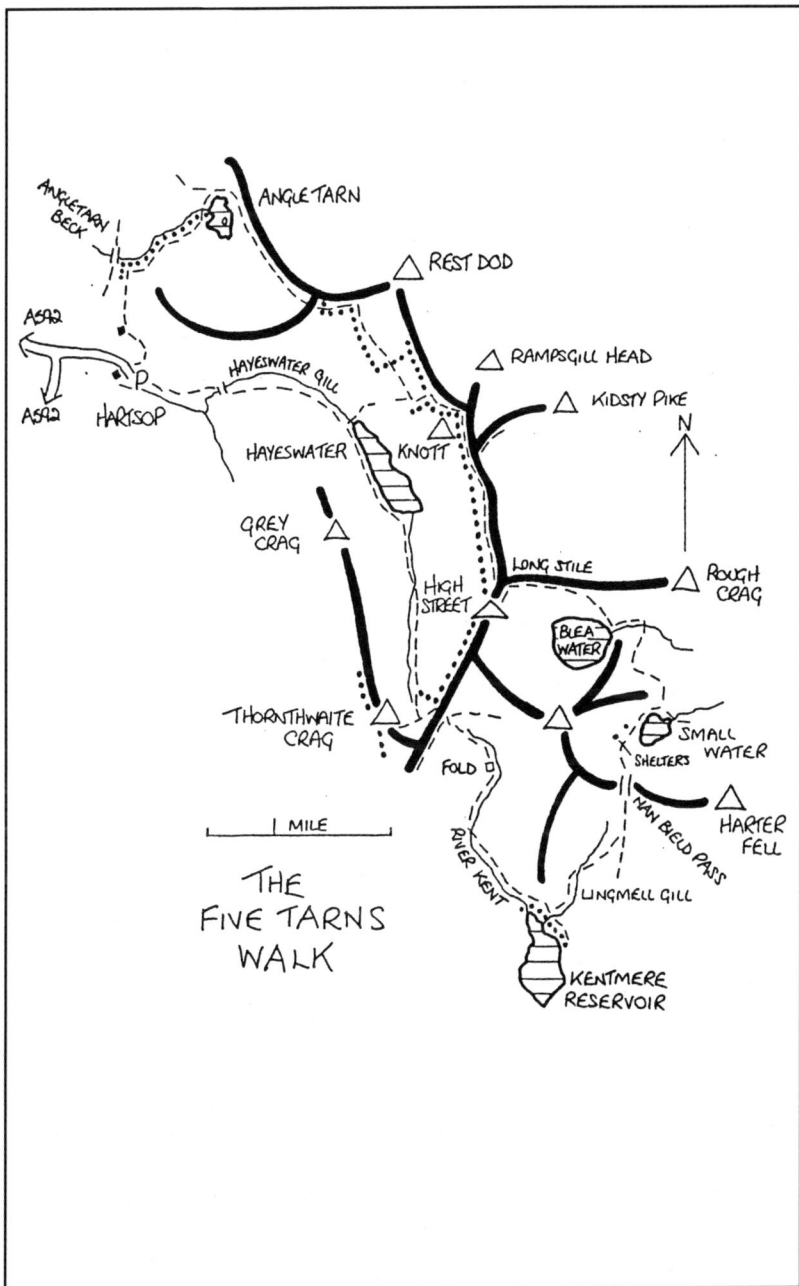

ANGLE TARN

ANKLETARN BECK

REST DOD

A592

RAMPSGILL HEAD

HAYESWATER GILL

KIDSTY PIKE

N

A592

HARTSOP

P

HAYESWATER

KNOTT

GREY CRAG

HIGH STREET

LONG STILE

ROUGH CRAG

BLEA WATER

THORNTHWAITE CRAG

FOLD

SMALL WATER

SHELTERS

HARTER FELL

NAN BIELD PASS

| MILE

RIVER KENT

LINGMELL GILL

THE
FIVE TARNS
WALK

KENTMERE RESERVOIR

Leave the path where it swings around the tarn and begins to climb. Follow a faint path left, behind and around a hummock guarding the tarn's north bank, to reach Angle Tarn Beck and its companion wall. Cross the beck, go through a gap in the wall, then turn right and descend alongside the wall. The route steepens into a rocky ravine, the path squeezing between crags and wall. It's rough underfoot in places, and steepish, and your knees, possibly feeling a bit blancmangy by now, might complain. The lower section is more wooded, but presently you emerge out of the vegetation on to a crossing path near a wall corner and stile.

Turn left along this path eventually to climb into a narrow passageway behind a house (Grey Rigg). Climb left now along a partially metalled track (your final climb, honestly), which levels then swings right and down into Hartsop. Beyond the gate turn left shortly to reach the carpark.

# HIGH STREET (NORTH–SOUTH)

**Walk 13**
**17 miles**
**4000 feet of ascent**

## Along the Roman Road – Pooley Bridge to Troutbeck

*For this one you need a car at either end, or to have arranged transport or accommodation. It follows a fine natural line and is not arduous, given reasonable conditions. On a sunny October day we did it in just over seven hours, including stops, and I became a Grandad four days later! The biggest climb is the eighteen hundred feet from Pooley Bridge to Loadpot Hill and that's spread over five miles. The terrain is mainly grassy, easy underfoot, though boggy in places. The three short sharp climbs over Froswick, Ill Bell and Yoke put a sting in its tail though. The views, naturally in lovely Lakeland, are superb and varied. Surely the most hard-bitten legionary must have paused in wonder. The 'road' avoids most of the summits but the proper fellwalker should not. I'll bet the Romans stepped aside to 'bag' the peaks. You don't conquer virtually all the known world by dodging the hard bits.*

*Parking: Pooley Bridge.*

FOLLOW the B5320 to the church. Turn right up the 'Howtown/ Martindale' road to a crossroads. Go straight on up the 'Roehead' road. The tarmac ends at a gate. Climb the track beyond to a cairn and a signpost 'Howtown/Roman Road' pointing right. Turn right to reach a stone circle 'The Cockpit'. The Romans probably sat in this eating their iron rations – tinned pizza!

Now follow a path bearing right, down to and across a beck. Beyond the beck it swings left to a cairn and a path fork. Bear left. At the next fork bear right towards the declivity of Aik Beck in the skyline ahead. The faint path swings right to the fenced mound of an underground reservoir. Climb left on to a cairned path leading to a smaller reservoir. Turn left along a faint path which leads to the first of two fenced reservoirs then disappears. Climb left, south, to emerge on to a sunken path – the Roman Road. Turn right and it begins to improve, and soon Loadpot Hill looms ahead. A quarry, Loadpot Hole, pocks its northern flank and it's thought that stone from it may have been used for the 'road's' foundations and kerb stones which have been unearthed hereabouts.

The 'road' skirts around the western flank of Loadpot Hill. Leave it and climb steeply left up a faint path on to the broad grassy summit of Loadpot Hill, 2201 feet, crowned by a trig-point. A small herd of wild ponies gambolled here on our last visit.

Continue beyond the trig-point, passing the foundations of a 'chimney' (2½" map) to join the 'road' again below Wether Hill. Follow it over Wether Hill, 2198 feet, a swampy lump whose cairned northern top appears the highest. Beyond Wether Hill the 'road' drops on to a boggy saddle before swinging right through a gap in a wall and climbing up onto the fence-crowned summit of Red Crag, 2332 feet. The cairn stands on the far side of the fence. Red Crag to High Raise is the most tedious part of the walk, a boggy plod between fence and a converging wall, passing the puddle grandiosely named Red Crag Tarn and crossing the hump of Raven Howe, 2358 feet, before climbing steeply up on to the rock-scattered summit of High Raise, 2361 feet. Now it gets interesting. The 'road' passes just to the west of this summit, so leave it and walk left to the cairn and neighbouring wind shelter.

Rejoin the 'road' and follow it down on to the grassy saddle below Rampsgill Head. Fork right to 'bag' this 2598 foot peak. Walk to its northern rim for a peep down on to some jagged rock towers and a gleam of Ullswater beyond the long strath of Martindale.

Now head south across broad grasslands to rejoin the 'road' on the rim of Riggindale. The great dome of High Street looms beyond. Let your imagination erase the wall and the walkers' worn paths, leaving only the 'road' twisting up around its west shoulder, and this is the view the legionaries saw over eighteen hundred years ago.

Thirteenth century cartographers called High Street the 'Brettestreete', or 'Street of the Britons', which infers that you could be walking one of the ancient highways of Britain. Well above two thousand feet for most of its length, it would be clear of the highest forest, which would mean fast travel and freedom from ambush. The Romans would be quick to grasp these advantages, although the thoughts of a raw 'sprog', fresh from the heat of the Med., sloshing his way across the dome in the teeth of a wet Lakleand spring 'sou-wester' must have been unprintable.

Turn right along the rim, then left down alongside the wall onto the Straits of Riggindale saddle. Climb between the wall and the fell rim. When the ground levels off, beyond the second rise, walk left to a cairn on the rim for the 'birds eye' view onto Blea Water, the deepest of Lakeland's tarns. Walk back to the wall and follow it up to the High Street trig-point at 2716 feet.

Descend southerly alongside the wall. Windermere's distant gleam hints that you've 'cracked it', but I wouldn't go as far as saying 'it's

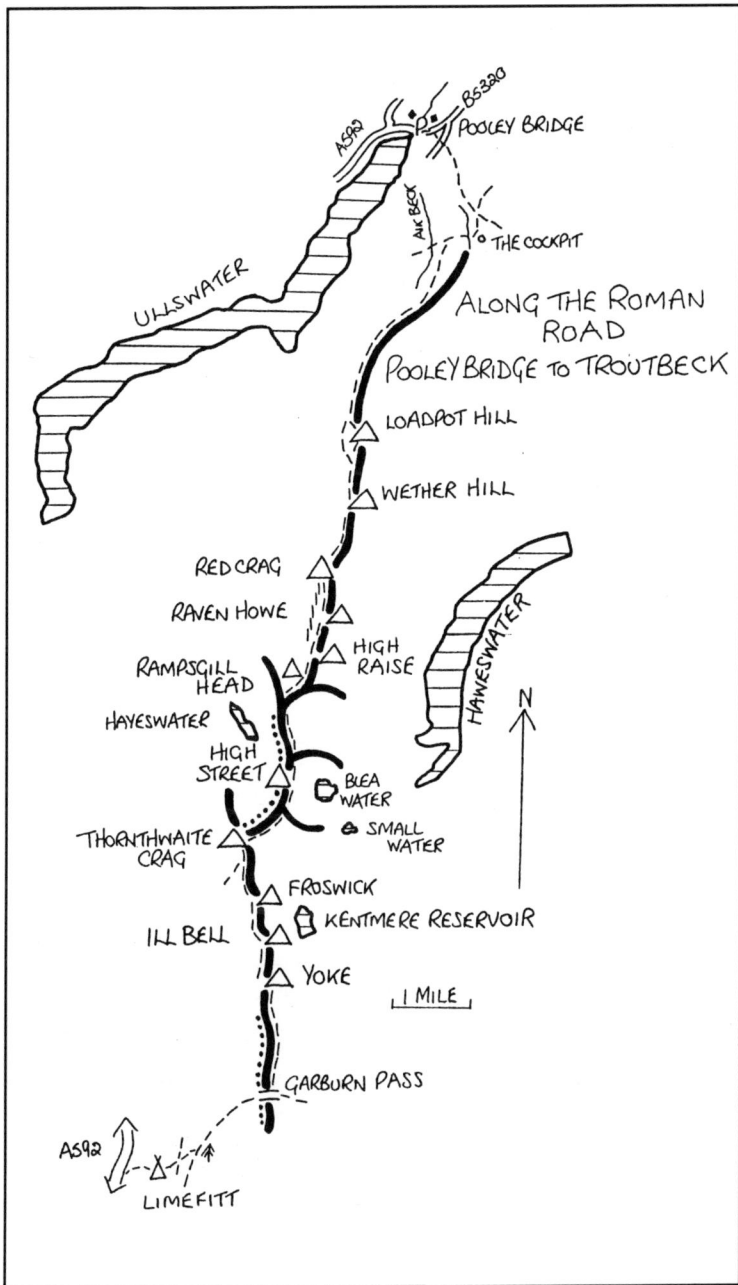

ALONG THE ROMAN ROAD
POOLEY BRIDGE TO TROUTBECK

downhill all the way'. From the wall corner fork south-west to swing around the rim of the Hayeswater combe and up to the fine finger of cairn gracing Thornthwaite Crag, 2572 feet.

Descend south-easterly alongside a tail of old wall and on down to a path fork marked by a sturdy fence-post embedded in a large boulder to rejoin the 'road' again. (Should you wish to follow the Roman Way over High Street rather than the fellwalkers' way, go through a gap in the wall on the Straits of Riggindale and climb its obvious line, passing about one hundred yards west of the trig-point, then down to breach a wall near a wall corner. From here the 'road' heads south-westerly across the east flank of Thornthwaite Crag to the fence post described.)

There's some doubt about the line of the 'road' from here on. It's argued that it descended into the Troutbeck valley by a spiralling track known locally as 'Scot Rake' and subsequently on to the Ambleside fort, or that it stayed high on the ridge, traversing across the western flanks of Froswick, Ill Bell and Yoke and on down to Garburn Pass and subsequently on to the Watercrook fort near Kendal.

Fellwalkers should be faced with no doubts about their route. It's a simple choice of up and down over the handsome crests of Froswick, 2363 feet, Ill Bell, 2483 feet, and Yoke, 2316 feet, to reach a stile straddling a wall corner. Cross the stile and follow the wall down on to the rough track crossing the summit of Garburn Pass. Turn right and down into the Troutbeck valley. Upon reaching a plantation on your left, look right for a stile just beyond a wall corner. Cross this and descend the steep fellside on to a crossing path close to a fork. Follow the lower path through a metal gate and turn right through a gap in a wall into the Limefitt Campsite. Walk through the site and up on to the A592.

# MARATHON

**46 miles
11,000 feet of ascent**

## The Lakes Threes

NOWADAYS it's called "The Lakeland Marathon" this circuit of the four highest mountains in England. The Ramblers' Association organises a mass attempt every summer, with feeding stations en route, mountain rescue teams on stand-by and certificates of merit awarded to all who compete the round in twenty-two hours or under.

Many years ago, in youth hostel common rooms, climbing club huts and the bars of those pubs patronised by the climbing/walking fraternity, it was simply known as "The Lakes Threes". There were no arbitary rules, but to start and finish at the same place and to complete the round in twenty-four hours or under was considered proper. Parties or individuals organised their own route and provisions and the only certificates of merit I ever saw presented were handwritten on thin narrow paper, perforated at regular intervals, with a phraseology that was somewhat obscene.

Although I personally dislike organised walks I should, I suppose, advise readers contemplating this 'marathon' to enter the organised event, for it would undoubtedly save them time and energy. Our three unsuccessful attempts and our final success were all badly planned and largely spur of the moment. As a result we suffered needless miles of walking and feet of climbing and a dire shortage of food and drink. Despite this, the achievement was all our own, a heartwarming memory that still produces rueful chuckles and reflex twinges of our thigh muscles.

The topography of Lakeland insists that the walks follows a fairly fixed route – few corners can be cut. Given below is a brief description of the route. Careful route planning is vital and those contemplating the walk should devote many hours poring over their 2½ inch maps, putting navigational flesh on the bare bones of this description. Assuming a start and finish in Keswick, begin by climbing up and down Skiddaw, 3054 feet, by the Jenkin Hill 'tourist' route. Then walk down Borrowdale to Seathwaite Farm. Climb one of the well-worn paths to Styhead Pass, either via Stockley Bridge or Taylor Gill Force. From Styhead Pass, link up with the Corridor Route and climb it as far as the Lingmell Col. From here, veer south, under Pike's Crag, into Hollow Stones, the bouldery combe below Scafell Crag. Pick your way across it and climb the scree fan issuing from the mouth of Lord's Rake. Climb Scafell, 3162 feet, by Lord's Rake, or the quicker but somewhat airier West Wall Traverse, which diverts left just below the first narrow col on Lord's Rake.

The quickest descent to Mickledore, from Scafell summit, is by Broad Stand. This is experienced scramblers' country, however, and if you aren't one it's safer to return to the foot of Lord's Rake by the way you came. Then climb along the base of Scafell Crag on to the stony ridge of Mickledore, where a well-trodden path climbs north-easterly across the boulder fields to reach the huge cairn crowning Scafell Pike, 3206 feet, the summit of England. Now follow yet another 'trade route' north-easterly, over Broad Crag and Ill Crag to reach that 'Piccadilly Circus' of mountain Lakeland, the wind-shelter below the crest of Esk Hause. Descend south-easterly to Angle Tarn.

Cross Angletarn Gill where it issues from the tarn and turn almost immediately left along a somewhat swampy path crossing the north-west flank of Rossett Pike before swinging east and down on to the saddle of Stake Pass. A tiresome thousand foot climb north-easterly brings you to the trig-point and cairn crowning High Raise. Head north over Low White Stones then north-easterly down on to the grassy saddle of Greenup Edge. Old rusting boundary posts can be a useful navigational aid over the last section. Turn right on Greenup Edge and descend into the swampy trough of Wythburn. Shortly below the pass and continue down the left bank of the gill, generally bearing east-north-easterly, well down into Wythburn before crossing the beck to join a good path on the far bank near a sheepfold. Follow this path down to emerge on to the road near Steel End Farm. Walk right to a junction with the A591. Immediately across the A591 a gate leads on to a 'permissive path' which leads left through the woods to emerge in the car park at the rear of Wythburn Church.

Climb Helvellyn, 3116 feet, by the 'tourist' path from Wythburn Church. Descend north-westerly from Helvellyn summit into the dip below Lower Man. Fork left here and follow the path descending along the rim of Brown Cove Crags and down to the car-park at the foot of Helvellyn Gill. All that remains now is around five wearisome miles along the verges of the A591 back to Keswick.